Simply Dedicated To Me

Spiders Jaguars & Lovely Mysterious Places of the Powerful Woman That is Me

Copyright © 2018 Orange NJ (L.T. Chase)

All rights Reserved. No part of this book may be reproduced or transmitted in any form or by any means without written permission from the author.

Library of Congress Number: 2018902434

ISBN: (978-0-692-07853-2)

WindChild Books LLC

Spiders
Jaguars
&
Lovely
Mysterious
Places
Of The
Powerful
Woman That is
Me

* Preface..
* Intro..

Poems

* Writers Block
* Essence Of The One
* Some Inner Expression for the Craving to Write
* Collision
* Words of Power
* Me
* A Weird Place In Time
* How You Do
* Root Chakra and Above
* Playin With Fire
* Flamingo
* Turtle Dreams
* Why Wait
* Heart's voice
* As Time Goes By
* Lovely, Lovely, Lovely
* Haikus
* Possibilities
* Spiritual Tidal Waves
* Deceived Love
* War Torn
* Ugly Monsters
* Sweet Black Tea
* Broken Glass
* Relations
* Boom Boom
* Spiders Jaguars & Lovely Mysterious Places of the Powerful Woman That Is Me
* Lovepoem

Preface

When I think of myself, I sometimes question the true nature of my Being. I find that when I ask, my higher self usually answers back. For a long time I would overlook or rather be afraid to trust what it would say to me over and over again. It is simply this:

"YOU ARE A CREATIVE SPIRIT."

But one might ask;"Well, if your higher self answered, what was the problem?" I'll tell you. I simply got caught up in what it is to be human. As humans, we have this passionate need to find a meaning to something. We ask over and over again, what does this mean or what does that mean? We get caught up in the "how" of things; and the big big one is worrying about what other people may say, based on *their* personal definition and interpretation of the world. But at the end of the day it's *their* meaning and only *their* meaning and it has nothing to do with you.

One may question why I am writing this or why do I feel the need to share my thoughts in a book of poetry...it's only a book of poetry! I will tell you why. It's because it's my truth and as Oprah Winfrey expressed in her acceptance speech at the 2018 Golden Globe Awards,"Your truth is the most powerful tool we all have."

I have wrestled with what it means to be a creative person. And I have resolved it to mean, **what ever the Divine energy of creation funnels your thoughts and hands into.** There are no limits and there are no boundaries. I used to get caught up in the saying: **JACK OF ALL TRADES MASTER OF NONE.**

It stopped me because I didn't want to be known as someone who was mediocre and insignificant in my creativity. I wanted to do it "right" and focus on one thing. However, it didn't work because my spirit liked to do many things. For example, I am musician at heart, a jewelry designer, a trained interior designer, a children's book author, a poet, soon to be novelist, and I love to dance. To add to this list, I'm a homeschool mom and a lyricist with a band. The point of this, is that for a long time I felt guilty and felt I had to choose. And because I felt I had to choose I was confused and frozen.

I no longer believe that. I no longer believe that because of the many examples of great *Creatives* that have proven this saying to be false. Gordon Parks comes to mind. His documentary Half Past Autumn exemplified the greatness of a person who allowed the creative force to be channeled where it needed to be at the moment.

Creative energy is creative energy! It comes from a Divine source. That energy is massive. That energy sometimes have to spill out into many things and sometimes it comes out in only one thing. We are meant to expand because that's what our Universe does everyday. It expands. It speaks. It has a desire to be heard and manifested through something. And when it doesn't get the opportunity to express itself it either festers, rots or explodes. And that's what I see for many of us *Creatives* who for whatever reason fail to speak our creative truths.

Fear can no longer stop us from speaking our creative truths. We can no longer worry if people will understand it, like it, care about it, or if we become famous (would be nice). We have to create because "it is what it is." And like Nature, we must create because if we didn't we would simply die (in some form or fashion).

I want to complete these words by saying our genius lies in our ability to express that which is unknown, not understood. Our genius lies in our ability to transform and to tell a story in such a way that it will touch move and inspire. Our genius lies in our ability to invent the impossible and solve a problem. It can do all of these things and at the same time bring justice to unjust thoughts and wrong doings through its creativity.
With this being said, I want to say thank you Dave Chapelle. Your creative comedic genius is heroic no matter how much you don't want to be a "hero".

Intro

Poetry can sometimes be so personal that it only has true meaning to the person who desperately needed to write it. But, with all things let out into the world, it becomes open to interpretation making it meaningful or meaningless to others.

I have no intention in forcing my words onto people's minds. I simply chose to share these poems that were manifested at the moment the creative source needed me to express them. For a long time I deeply felt no desire to publish any of the poems I have written throughout my life. I didn't see the point. But one day my spirit shouted out to publish a small book of poetry…and this time I didn't question.

The title of the book came to me in the most rarest of moments, while standing at my kitchen counter. I heard it in my mind and knew that it came from a spiritual place. Spiders and jaguars are powerful animal symbols that I will leave up to the reader to interpret what it means for them.These poems are in no particular order and 90% of them were written in my early twenties. I went through my storage box of poems and picked out poems my spirit immediately said *"yes"* to.

I have no idea what will come of this book of poetry but I do want it to touch someone. Also, I have to say that in publishing these poems, a strong feminine energy radiates within me. I feel empowered in some strange way.

So if this message from the Universe to publish this book of poetry adds somehow in someway to the power of the Divine Feminine, then I am grateful and happy to have listened.

This book is for me and anyone else who feels they have lovely mysterious places. Live in the Light!

-L.T. Chase

Writer's Block

I find myself struggling to bring forth words,
words used to compose melodies in songs
sentences in books
And lines found in poetry and rhyme

I try to say something
But the words are strangled lifeless like stillborn
growing for nothing.
Just like the nothing that comes from the end of
this pen

But as they say better late than never
Enough of this rambling tho! Cause all it is is the
clearing of clutter, the clearing of chaos to create
the clearing to write something! To touch move and
inspire me and others

So until then I'll marinate on this writer's block
unashamed cause every writer has their day where
they, like myself, find themselves struggling to
bring forth words like those used to compose
melodies in songs, sentences in books
And lines found in poetry and rhyme

Essence of the One

I don't want to think

I just want to know

Thinking contaminates the essence of the One

I don't want to think

I want to know beauty

Know imagination

Know creativity

Not think about it

Just know about it and in that is a freedom from opinions, thoughts, and rules of others brought about from what they thought, not knew...

Divinity

Some Inner Expressions of the Craving to Write

Nature's rising doesn't give you time to react if you are slow in wit or lack consciousness of what it is or what it's all about

Some may say "The hell with Nature!" which undoubtedly is a way of damning the truth. The truth that be you, that be we, that be all

I can sit all day forever writing poems of such ambiguity
and it wouldn't make a difference if I knew for sure of what I speak because the sun will rise the sun will set
the moon will appear and be illuminated during the ignorance of the day

The gases we breath will still be needed between us and the trees and the birds will fly and women will still shed light and manifest that which consists of all elements-with the help of her counterpart that is, which inevitably brings us back to completeness

You know what I speak of and if you don't then quick, familiarize yourself with three, six, and zero otherwise known as the number nine

And as I said earlier, I can sit all day forever writing what I'm not sure of and even in that there is a truth
And with all this madness in the world what other method do we have but the truth

No matter how far fetched it may sound It can't sound as far fetched as the shit that's going down

Someone lied who told you that ignorance is bliss ignorance is the bane of our modern day existence Where does it get us? Get my point?

The truth shall set you free That is what's real
And in the words of the Last Poets
What I'm gone do? What you gone do?

What I'm gone do is reach for understanding.
Demand your own soul and not what He demands

Cause if you don't know have mercy on your soul cause Nature's rising doesn't give you time to react if you are slow in wit or lack consciousness of what it's all about.

Collision

I sat at the top

of my seat between thought and confusion

and felt that

if I thought any less things would

spring into being

And then I realized

I may be right so I sat at the back of my seat

and let thought and confusion collide

Words of Power

Djehuty speaks, my heart cries out
stories told, untold, denied, and ignored
Of goals and visions of what life should
be like for us—-Women/Wombmen
honored, revered, loved and acknowledged

Djehuty speaks, my heart cries out
stories told, untold, denied, and ignored
laying heavy on our life creating the dis-ease
we feel manifested in physical meltdown…
spiritual trauma… absence of true self

Me

This isn't what you think it might be, a cliche poem about possibilities between two people three four or all or how the trees are beautiful and the sun making flowers grow—-This is about Me!

It's about what I want, how I want it,
when I want it
Its about how I feel when I'm feeling how I feel
It's about expressing Me with no apologies
It's about looking how I look when I choose to look a certain way, mismatched colors or hair in a frenzy
It's about doing what I want when I want to do it
It's about getting what I want when getting what I want is important

My grandmother always said to me to always be happy and even though she's not here with me in body, I know in spirit she can always see me

I said it before and I'm gonna say it again this poem is sure enough not what you thinkin
This—poem—is—about me!

It's about crying the blues when the blues get too blue and being simple when complexities get too complex

No explanation of why I'm the way I am just feeling free in being lil ole me! All the good and even the bad just being me without feeling guilty

See I'm gonna say it again cause I don't think you understand it's about me right now and who I am No Apologizing!

Cause this isn't what you think it might be a cliche poem about possibilities between two people three four or all or how the trees are beautiful and the sun making flowers grow—-This is about Me!

A Weird Place In time

I am what I'm not right now
in this place, in this realm.

I am what I'm not right now
And what I'm not, I will soon be

Sooner than the bird's chirps greet the morn
and an earthworm drowning from the rain
Sooner than the earth completes it's journey

Beginning where I'm not right now
But oh how soon I will be!

How You Do

Laughter is a blessed event
when it comes from your lips that speak my name
And with that same breath, tickles my hips

Now is this to say that laughter is
only blessed when it comes from you?

No, the only time I call it blessed is
when you do it how you do

Root Chakra and Above

Just before rain, the earth bleeds of scents
unlike any other a ritual of sexual ripening
A preparation of sensual ecstasy
The earth moans with the sounds of melodic voices
in the wind

She succumbs overwhelmed by her expectancy
she lay open and her joy spreads touching every
corner of existence seizing our senses manipulating
our movements from rigorous jolts of our daily
strain to movements of serenity dancing with
sacred spirits of her hidden realms

Just before rain the sky darkens,
a blanket of privacy a matter of security
ensuring this coming together of water and earth
The sun closes its eye, flowers bow their heads
the birds provide the melodies
transforming hearts, transforming reasons to exist
Visions of pink light shedding into blue
melting into green absorbing into gold are
these transformations but of the soul

Playin With Fire

Awakening!!!
Fire suppressed
Released!!!
Backdraft!!!

Watch out! What's this! Desire?
Haven't seen you for a long time
Now reacquainted, catching up for lost times
But question is, why now? Dare I ask?
Dare I inquire?

Fire more intense
should I shake hands? embrace? what?
Maybe best to acknowledge from afar

But fire can be tricky; spreads; intensifies
left alone can dwindle down to ash
Remnants of what once was
Who knows? There's moments when I just don't care!

But playin with fire will definitely burn
So playin could never be an option

Flamingo

What would happen if
you touched my skin
and singed my entire body
Only to find you have healed me
And burned away the parts of me
that were useless and a hinderance

What would happen if I rejoiced
in this fire of sorts and danced like the
flamingo from the flame

Turtle Dreams

Today I wept my most sincerest weep
Too deep for me to understand too deep
Only the crust of earth's soil can share my pain
Stripped of life caressed by rain

Today I wept though in a distant place
The memories burned my inner self
but dared not show on my face

I tried so hard to smother the struggling
life of this spirit memory
But with my wall of pride shattered the pain
seeped through and it no longer mattered

Today I wept my most sincerest weep
the thought of you who was not destined to keep
But my heart's curiosity lay shaded by this fact
hoping to manipulate this predetermined
natural pact

So I weep with remembrances like elephant mind
begging soaring eagle to leave this behind
transcending me to powers higher to command
myself from envisioning the two of us same

butterfly clan

Though the beauty of our colored wings would radiate the sun, dreaming of turtles we may never be one
so I fight to break free from the one not destined to keep for today I wept my most sincerest weep

Why Wait

I couldn't see the forest past the trees
So I stood waiting for some mighty wind
to part them so I can see enough to walk
through

But now I see that the mighty wind is me
So I can no longer stand waiting!

Heart's Voice

In all this world
We have the one thing
that lets us know we
are still connected
to the Source

It is the voice
channeled from
the heart and
when the heart
speaks we must
listen to its voice

No fear of...
No doubt about...
Just listen because
when its voice
stops speaking is
when we are no longer
connected to the Source

And when that happens
we may find we are miles
away from our mission

Whether we know what it is
or not

Enjoy speaking your
voice but don't forget
to listen to its heart

As Time Goes By...

Innocence,
like a child's laughter
when not present, brings rot
to a once fresh environment
Brings despair and dulls the eyes of visions once
bright and colorful, clogs the ears of music once
sweet and melodious, hardens the heart preventing
exuberant life

Innocence
in its natural state, when untouched
sees the world like one would a fantasy
impossible possibilities possible
It's a beautiful vibration, touching all those near
It's a flower that blooms to maturity in its own
time, not forced from its garden

Cause innocence, like death, once its gone
it's forever gone, no coming back
The memories of its pleasures, its blessings, leaves
a nostalgia and at times, a longing to return to a
place only babies have the honor of experiencing

And through their eyes we relive and remember
what innocence looked and felt like back
when we were untouched, unscarred
And loved from a place that becomes tainted
as time goes by

Lovely, Lovely, Lovely

Lovely is the word
Lovely is the word that flows off my tongue that's
been on my mind
a mind that speaks lovely

Lovely is the voice of a mother who envelops
you in the hopes and dreams of You
lovely like wishing for cherry lollipops
demanding to be wanted by its magnificent lure

Lovely is the thought of birds flying above the
rainbow and seeing the clouds aligned with sequin
studded traces of your dreams like tender drops of
wonder that elegantly carries this very moment

Lovely is the heart that's willing to feel love,
endure pain, speak the truth, and bow down to
vulnerability

Lovely is little girls jumping rope and disagreeing
at the same time and lovely is that little girl in you
still dreaming today

Haikus

<u>Elysian Fields</u>
coming together
peaceful journeys of the rain
contentment is mine

<u>Imagination</u>
panic state of mind
rapture of the crocodile
leaving land alone

<u>Higgledy Piggledy</u>
cephalic torment
running far towards the wind
expecting nothing

<u>Clarity</u>
wrinkled chains of thought
steam iron pressured smoothness
flow like waterfalls

Lessons
reaching upper age
divinity of the times
wisdom long acquired

Innocence
carnival laughter
chocolate skin eyes glowing
remembered moments

From One Ear To Another
sitting drinking tea
old/new friend discussing times
one more day to come

Colored Love
purple yellow blue
green in between you and me
a sigh tells it all

Possibilities

In my mind
possibilities flourish
like rain replenishing dry lands once forgotten
where blossoms of strawberries invade the air with
pungent scents of sweetness
where bees, hypnotized, forget their sting nestling
on a passerby's arm

In my mind
possibilities flourish
bringing smiles upon my face of various degrees
constructing geometric shapes
of maybe some earth shattering cosmic force
that may exist
An example to the masses that chances are…….

For in my mind
possibilities flourish
symbolizing truths to be told to ourselves accepting
unfathomed thoughts
Now clear as pink lights shining into that place
we often keep dark and for all we know
yearning to be illuminated

Spiritual Tidal Waves

I move!
I move to rhythms!
rhythmic rhythms!
vibrations vibrating
I move to swaying trees, leaves rustling in pushing winds
I move to pattern tones of my voice- when its lyrical- when it flows, I move!

I move to pressure-point being I move!
I move to light, photogenic light
inspiring spiritual tidal waves
I move, yes to green…I move yes to blue…
I move yes to yellow.. I even move
to you! to you! to you!
I even move to me, When I'm flying high above mounds of almonds-eagle spread wings

I move to his touch—-to his melodic tone abyss moving me deep from within
I move to joyous cries howling wolves—- I move!
I move to open floor empty space to dance of course!

I move to sudden combustion of noise—- damn real I move!

I move in circles… I move in prisms…
Well if you really must know, I move because I'm Woman! Natural moves from the beginning to end I move with life inside-moving!
I move through tears and anyway you can fathom
I move squirming…crawling… jumping… hopping… running and walking. And when it comes to seduction,
let's just say- Phenomenal! Causing solids to liquify

I move to drums! I move up, down, side to side backwards, forwards, in swarms I move!
Like rotating fan blades keeping you satisfyingly cool

I move like rays beaming, causing life to bloom
I move to rain dropping, thunder clapping, lightning striking. I am a walking, talking,
cry when I have to, strut when I want to, growing, breathing, rhythmic vessel. Moving is my life!

Deceived Love

Like sinking hearts...ablated imago
Like an illegible canard that otherwise had you
blissfully happy

Like denied sincerity the cacophony of loud
laughter of the callowness of your trust
Like the death of a newborn, potent with
possibilities...illusive abundance

Like cardiac arrest...emotional depletion
Like the shocking last thought of an entangled
spider's prey...broken ankles unable to run from
danger

Like an earthquake opening your earthly
foundation and swallowing it whole
A blow to your gut, the warning feeling you twice
ignored

Like the word NO! the piercing sound of ballyhoo
Like a caged cheetah's speed inhibited...foul play on
your hearts content...Painful spasms
Like what happened to Hughe's dream deferred

ground where now lies that last piece you craved, yearning evermore!

Like the death of Caesar and his realization, "E tu, Brute?" Tap shoes dancing on thin ice, Mars disguised as Venus, Mother publicly slapping your face!

Like severed lines, communication suspended curiosity wails, dire emergency ignored

Like sitting through a bad movie paying the cost despite. Sipping hot chocolate burning your tongue

Like wild game hunted despite the chance of extinction…Pain of Daddy leaving

Like a homeless child fostered by the streets, the intrusion of a tapeworm causing you to feel empty Putting your Siamese to sleep and watching it watch you as it takes its last breath

Deceived love a sacrificial act of an otherwise sacrosanct jewel.

War Torn

She be war torn apart
Stripped...Lost
Lost in the brush and weeds of sacrifice and compromise of sacrifice and pain of sacrifice and mourn

She be filled with battle scars not made on the fields of battle but on the fields of life...on the fields of giving. Giving and giving again, returning with no medals, no ribbons, just memories of sacrifice and the neglect of what she needed for her Woman self...Her Girl self!

No return of the reverence due
That soft sensual feminine place that stood in the shadows given no cue to shine just standing in the shadows of sacrifice.

And in her place stood the Warrior who took the blows and fought until it became hardened and stiff and tired just war torn, ready to take a break if only for a moment to let that Woman...that Girl... that Feminine softness, Feminine tenderness, take its turn setting free this prisoner of war.

Freedom they both feel, The Warrior...The Woman Soft. And for this she weeps taking long awaited deep breaths. Freedom to truly BE...No big bad presence to dominate

She be war torn but survivor nonetheless.
She be war torn but survivor nonetheless

Ugly Monsters

I look at monsters right before my eyes showing their ugly ways revealing their nasty intent

And I don't blink because their faces were disguised as you...Someone I know... Someone I've known for many cycles

Wasn't afraid of these monsters because I would play with them. Laugh with them. share my body with them, make plans with them for the future of till death do us part

Ugly...Ugly...Ugly monsters making friends with me disguised as you Chocolate brown masculine skin Making promises you never could really keep of being lovers bound by a ring of eternity now with collected dust stifling its energy chocking its power of forever

I look at monsters right before my eyes showing their ugly ways revealing their nasty intent and I don't blink because their faces were disguised As you...As you...As you

Sweet Black Tea

Sweet Black tea
I sit sipping in hopes to bury this navy blue like
blues that sits heavy below the surface of my
otherwise nonchalant behavior

I sip trying to create the feeling that you actually
are here holding me in your arms, speaking my
language of touch and spending time

But you're not so I sip my eighth cup, I imagine
that it's you telling me you never want to leave
But you're not and I am alone, dreaming of big
dreams of me somewhere in the future smiling,
laughing, loving…being held by someone
not being alone

I ache from this navy blue like blues that subtly
shapes my face, ache my bones, altering the way I
move, the way I speak, the way I see myself-
ultimately the way I feel

Funny cause you appear to be a bright sunny yellow radiant as if the blues never had a chance to entertain the thought of visiting your space
What is that?

I dare not speculate, my blues may then turn obsidian black and that will no longer be the blues it would be something else, I dare not go there I have things to finish...mending to do...

Hard though! To tend to these when this navy blue like blues has been pulling my puppet strings
What a mess!

So I sit here sipping on my sweet black tea trying to reconstruct that warm fuzzy feeling of worth, gentle touch, from masculine hands, holding me and never letting go and me never letting him go

But I sit sipping... sipping... sipping my sweet black tea until there is no more...Damn!

Broken Glass

Broken glass!
On the floor like thousands of pieces of angry
emotions. Sharp! Jagged! waiting for prey
waiting for anyone happening to walk by
Shattered upon the floor dropped by a careless
hand not quite realizing its value...it's beauty

There it lay once a whole work of art, a rarity
now laying upon the floor into a thousand little
pieces of angry emotion...of grief stricken glass

Is there any way to be put back to itself?
Is there anyone with an artful hand to do
so..Maybe not

A beautiful work of art now laying upon the floor by
a careless hand whose handling was not worth the
responsibility. Carried it with no care...threw it in a
bag...any ole bag! No protection. No fragile sign. No
indication of its value. Now broken on the floor like

Thousand of pieces of angry sad emotions...
Thousands of pieces of angry sad emotions...
Thousands of pieces of angry sad emotions...

Relations

And then I realized
In order to get back to me, I had to stop thinking
of myself in relation to you, cause then I'll be
almost nothing

Defining myself in relation to you, I was dull,
almost lifeless standing in the shadow of love
for myself

But here I am after years of blind, displaced,
powerless definitions of all the woman I became to
believe was true; after the kicking, screaming and
resistance of this one simple revelation

That in order to get back to the powerful, sensual,
beautiful, creative, special Woman that I am,
I had to stop thinking of myself in relation to you

Boom Boom

Do you think or do you feel?
And which one do you think is more important?
Just might have created a contradiction did you catch it? Did you feel it? Am I confusing you? Maybe I am confusing myself.

boom ladeedadeedaboom boom boom ladeedadeedaboom

Just some music to fill the blank space that most people won't admit they do in the privacy of their mind

Again, I ask do you think or do you feel?
which one has more weight…more significance
Bet you pick the wrong one and yes, how dare I tell you what's the right or wrong thing!

boom ladeedadeedaboom boom boom ladeedadeedaboom

I'm back is this causing you to feel a certain way or think a certain way depends on which one you picked though…You see what I'm saying?

left brain right brain which one is supposed to be the dominant and which one is suppose to be recessive.

Leave it to me I'll be inclined to choose the side that lines up with the maternal side of me-feminine side-right side. Though those that think would disagree and think that their disagreeing is more correct dismissing feelings and intuition dismissing feelings on the belief that that's for out of control women who let their emotions get out of control therefore making feeling obsolete... hmmmm let's think about that...

boom ladeedadeedaboom boom boom ladeedadeedaboom

Returning from thinking, I mean feeling I mean well anyway thought about it and I feel it's all wrong. Right side just might be the right side to everything-you feel me?

boom ladeedadeedaboom boom boom ladeedadeedaboom

*Spiders Jaguars & Lovely Mysterious Places of
The Powerful Woman That Is Me*

look into my eyes
do you see the deep secret places that want to tell
all of its mysteries?

do you dare to place yourself inside my worlds
worlds that's never been seen or truly fathomed
I walk with these mysteries, some beyond even my
knowing, a pandoras box of magic and what it is to
be truly free, where witches' brews are a common
drink

look into my eyes do you feel the power
like jaguar jaws I devour, enter if you must, this
secret mysterious place screaming to be known but
best kept hidden-for your sake!

I dance upon my weaved web of dreams and
sacred knowings, seductively embracing this
powerful mysterious place that only spiders and
the divine feminine understand

Love Poem

If yesterday became today, I would forever be in the present moment; in the middle of God's eye; in the seat of love. I would *Be* love if yesterday became today.

If yesterday became today, mistakes would be short lived and my compassion for all would stand at the seat of my Being...at the core of my heart. I bow to the majesty of life. I bow to the grace of love. I bow to the humility of nothingness and to the gratefulness of everything. I surrender to love; to its power, to its force, to its light. But my awakening is not enough. Love needs the surrender of All, the loyalty of hearts and the obedience of souls. It needs vulnerability just like the sun willing to rise everyday to give its heart and warmth. Never taking just Being in love in its state of truth to its nature.

Love, just like the air existing in plain sight but unseen to the closed heart. Never mind the mind it has no true power in this realm. Can we see this? Can we accept this? And if love is still in need today, then tomorrow may never need to wonder if hate will continue its reign. Open your heart. Unlock your bound soul to the love of God to the love that is you. Isn't this one in the same? Isn't this beautiful? isn't this Divine? Start with compassion for yourself then to others. Forgive yesterday's shortcomings. forgive life's hardballs. Fill it with surrender. Be in the moment that is the Truth. Yesterday... Today... Tomorrow... becomes one.

If yesterday became today, I would forever be in the present moment; in the middle of God's eye; in the seat of love. I would Be love. You would Be love. We would Be love. Say you will...Yes...Yes... Yes!!!

www.ingramcontent.com/pod-product-compliance
Lightning Source LLC
Chambersburg PA
CBHW072038060426
42449CB00010BA/2336